Kittens and Puppies

Colouring Book

Adult Coloring Books

Aryla Publishing 2019

978-1-912675-47-0

www.arylapublishing.com

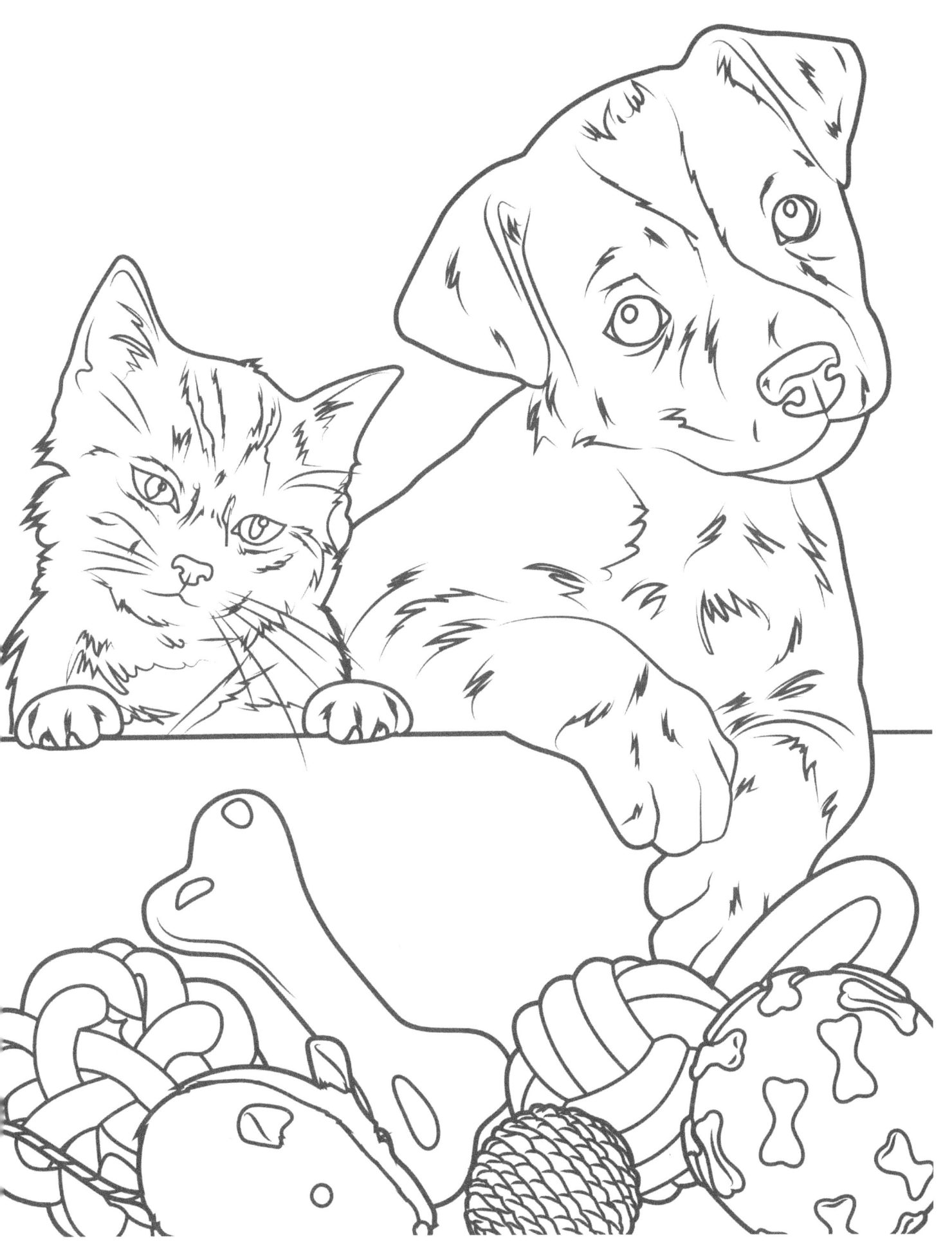

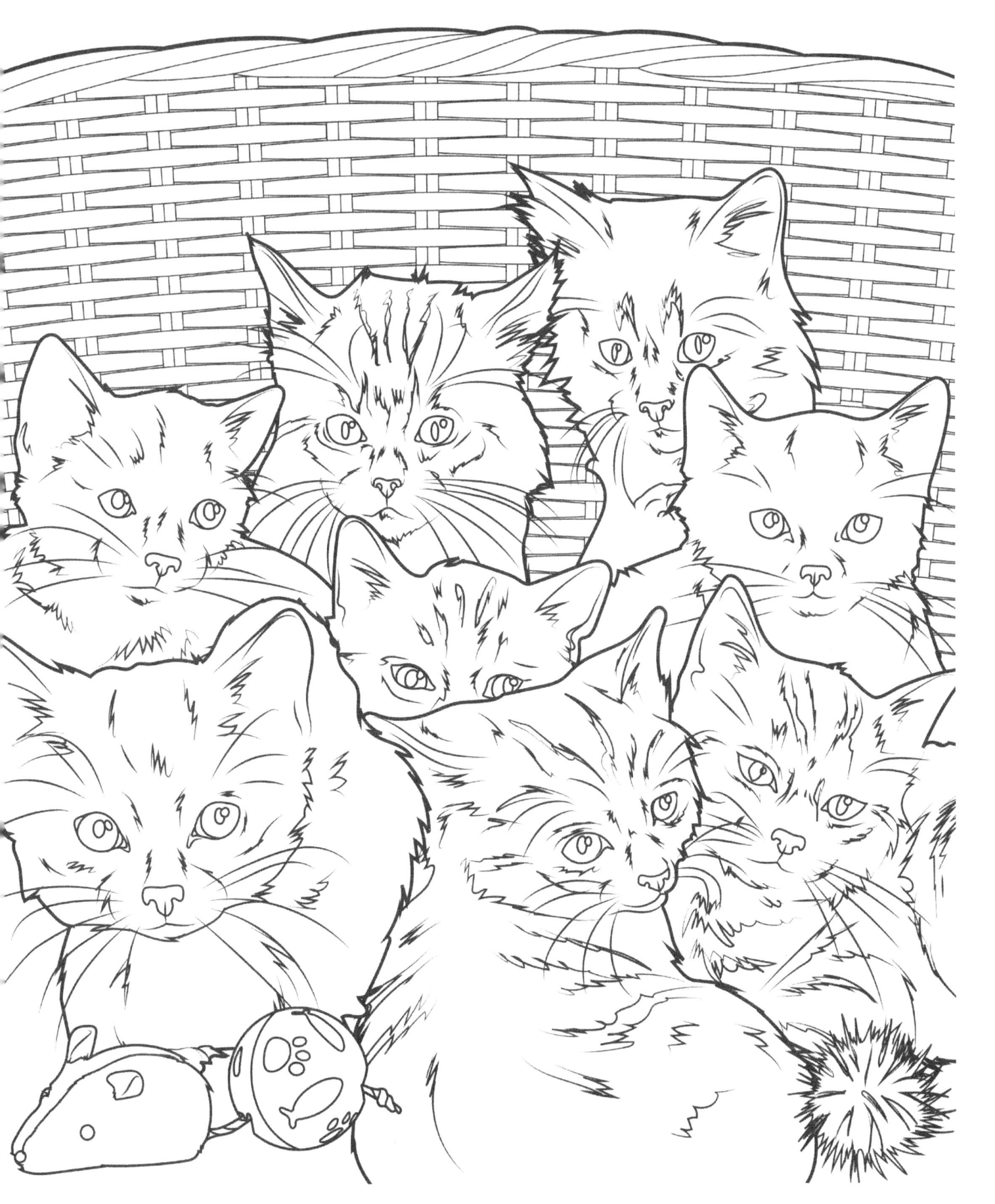

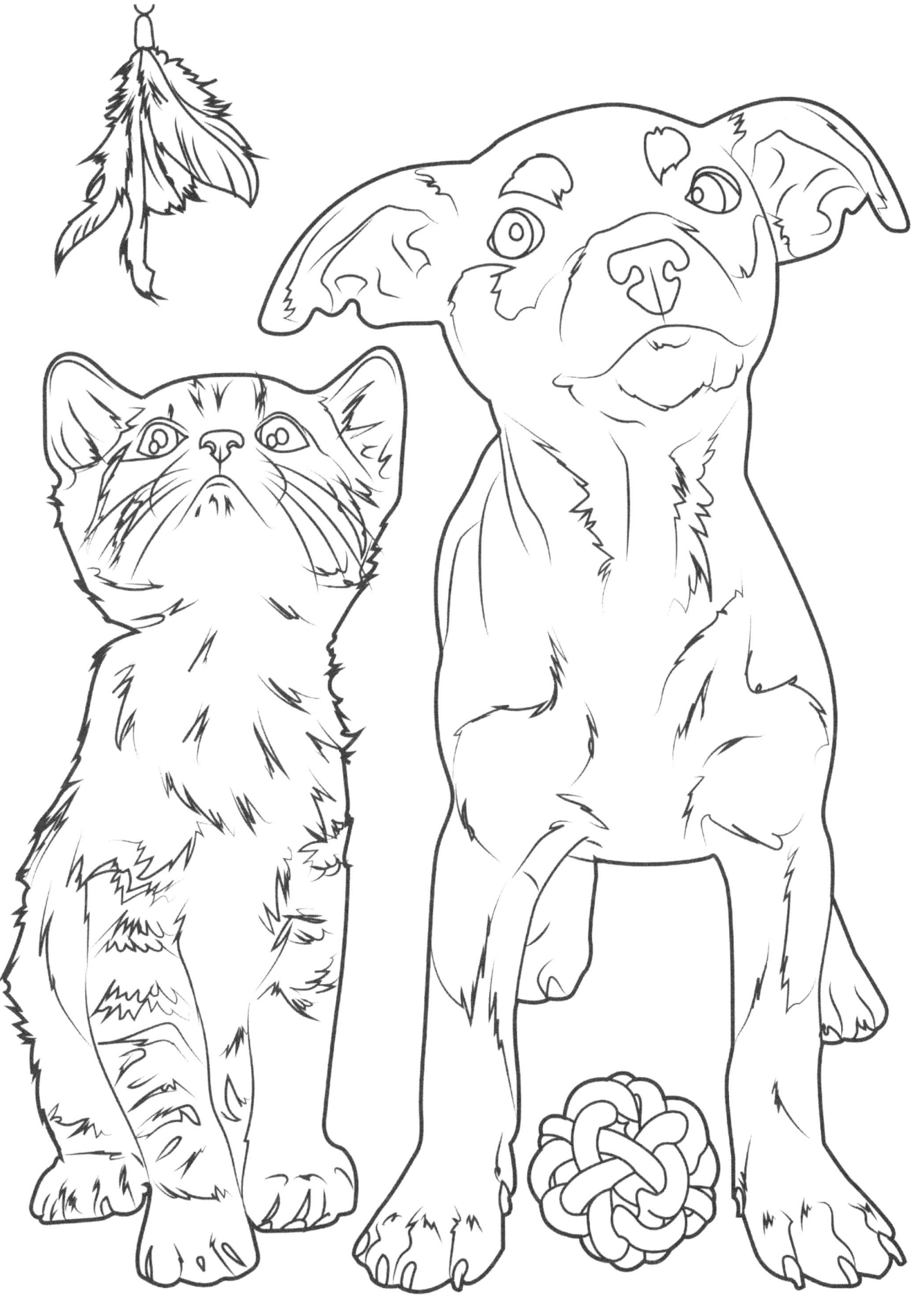

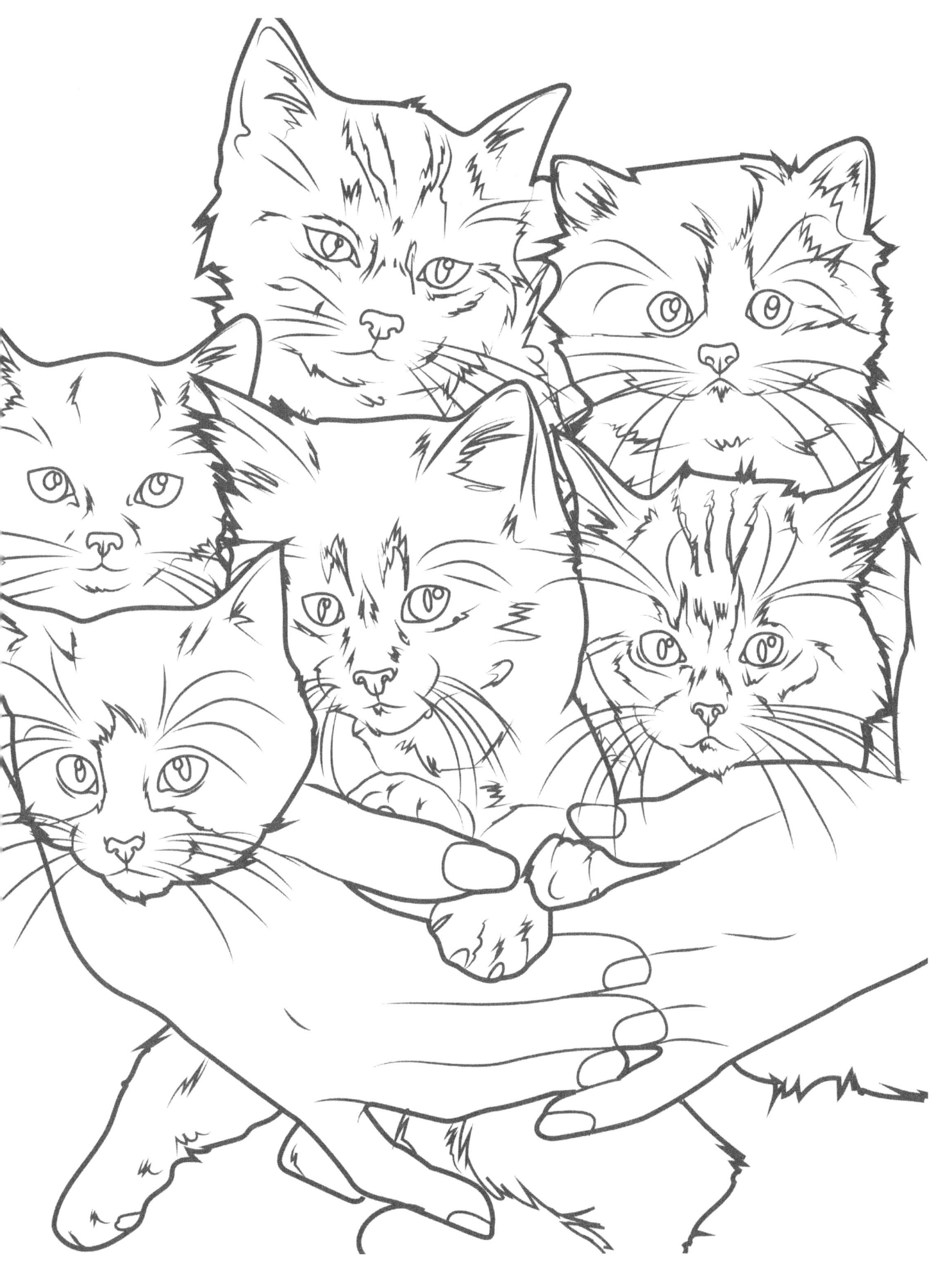

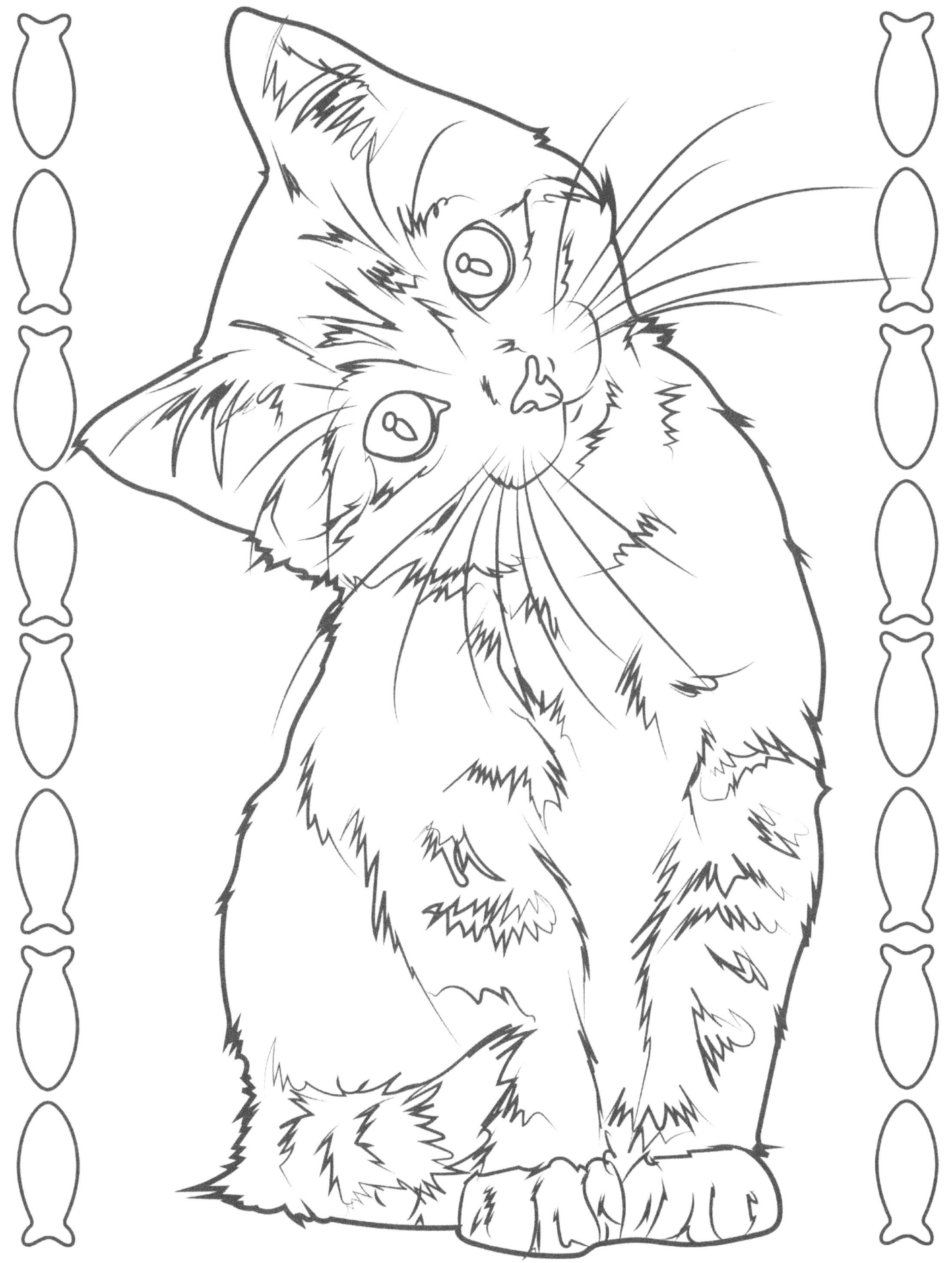

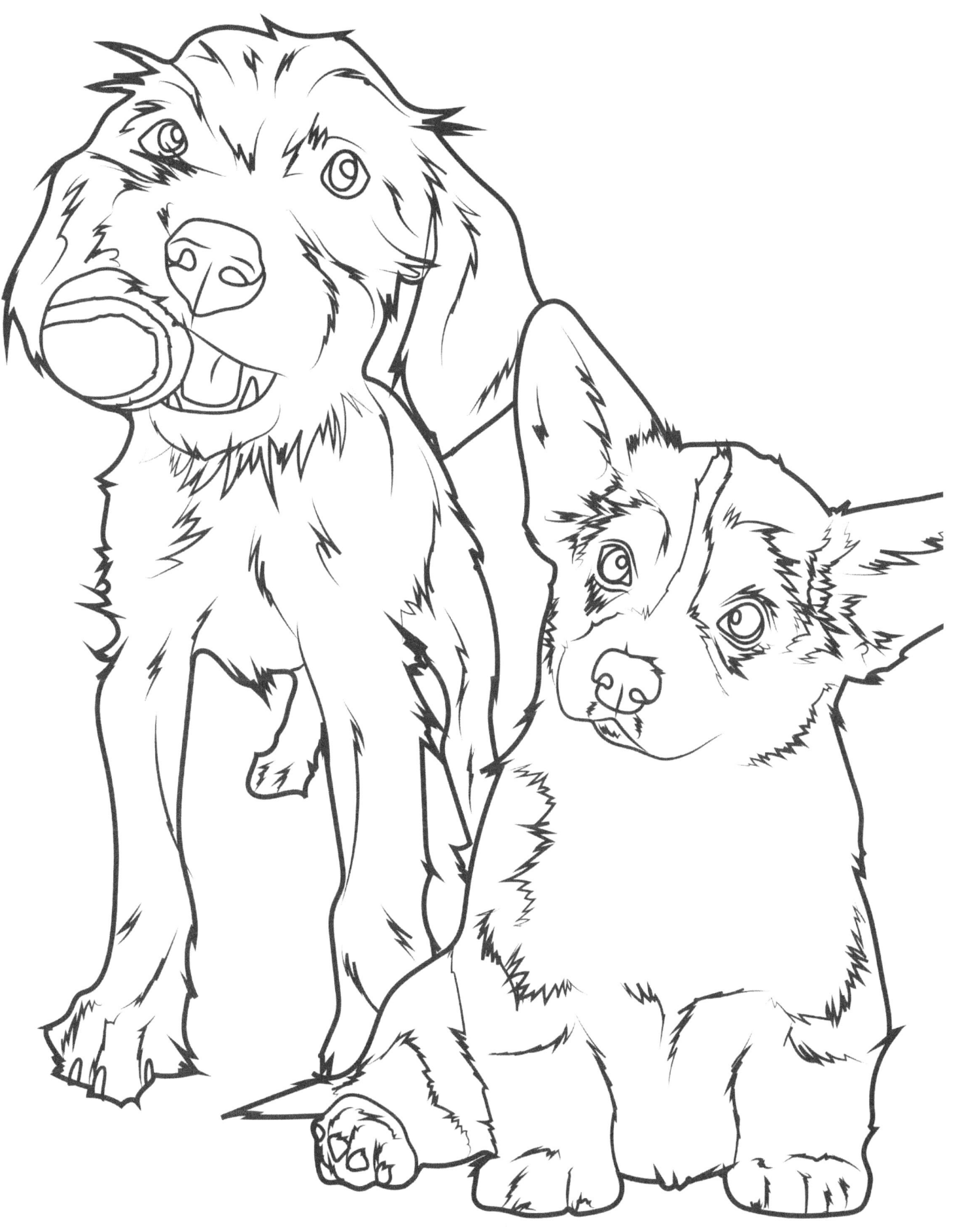

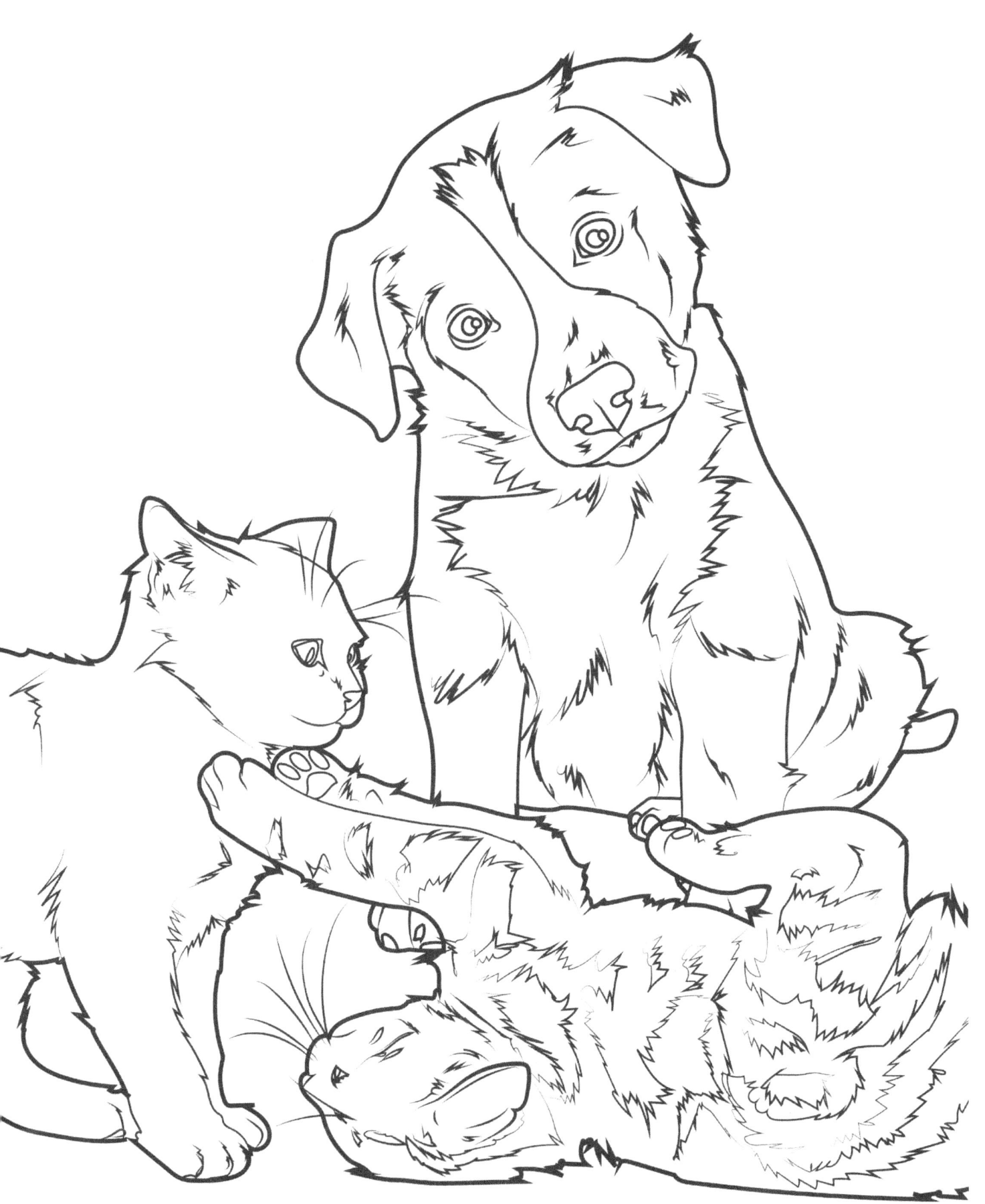

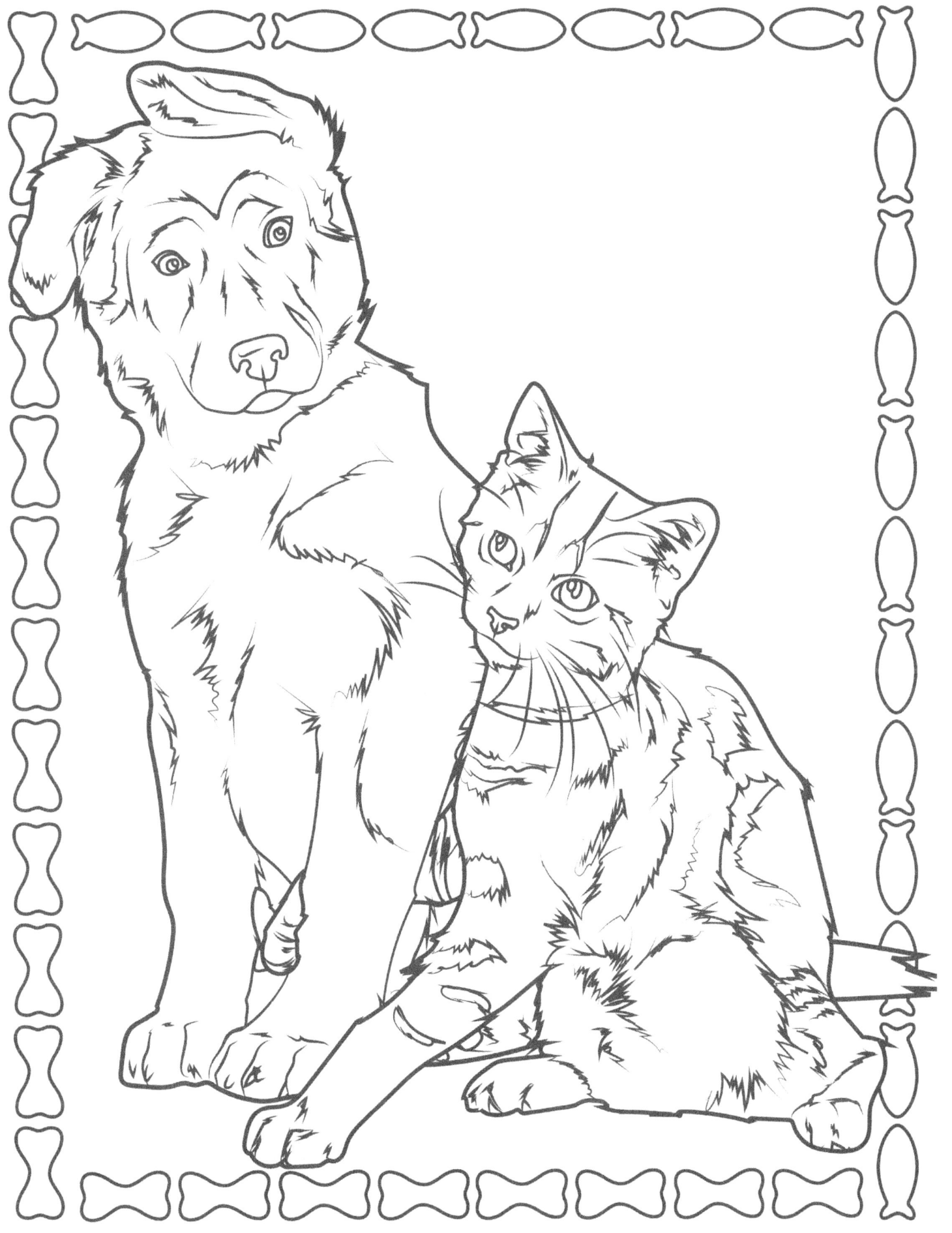

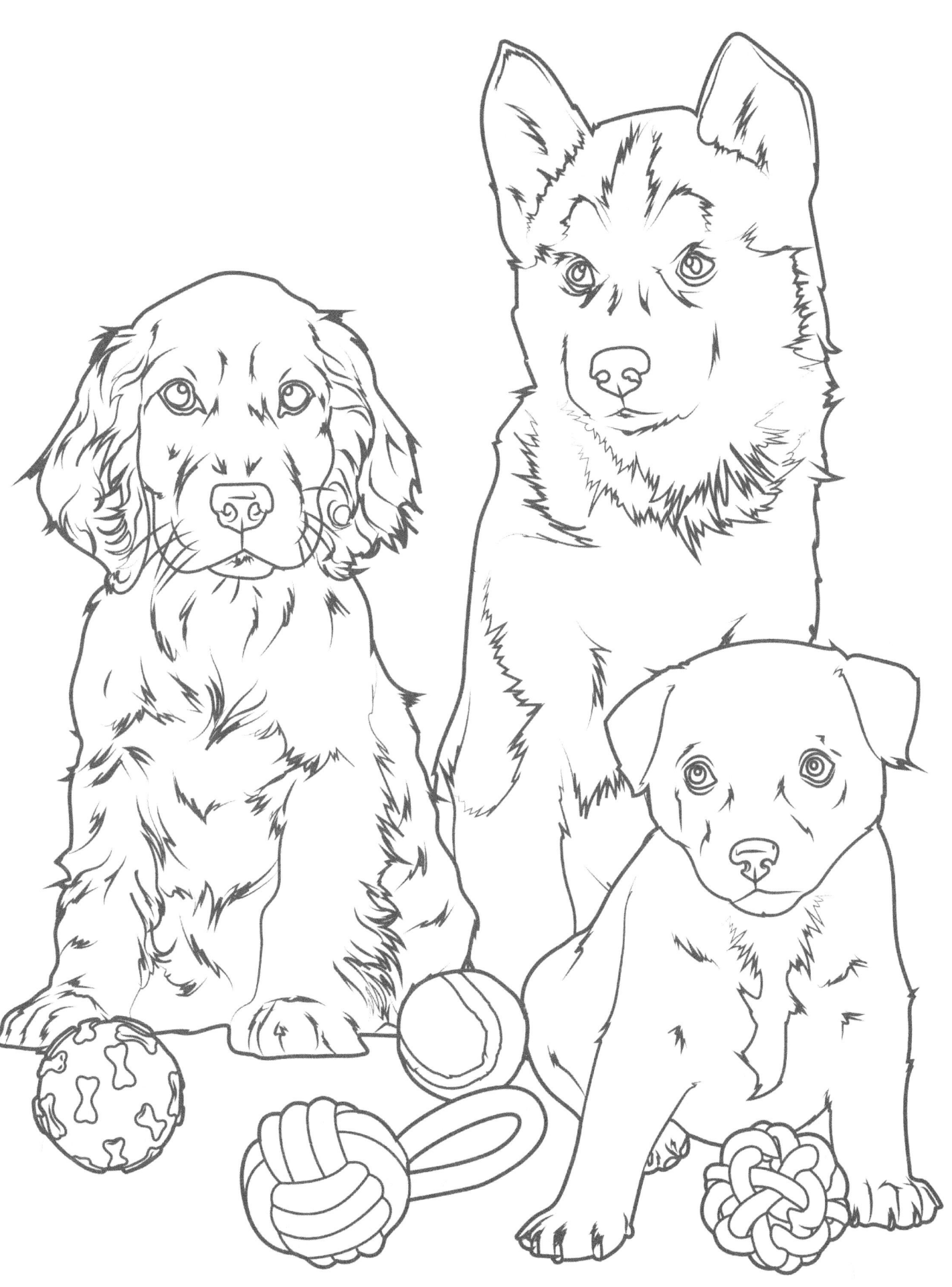

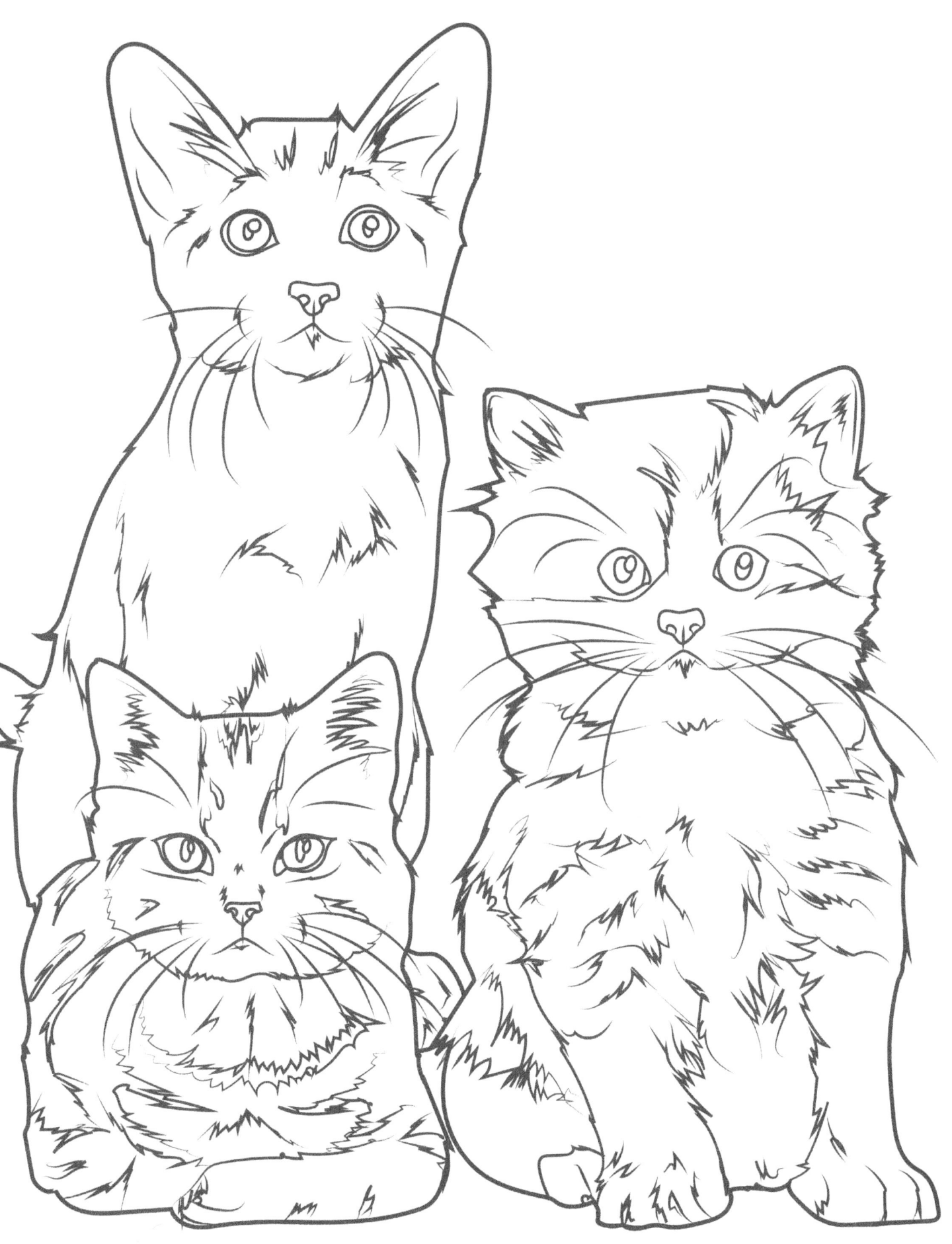

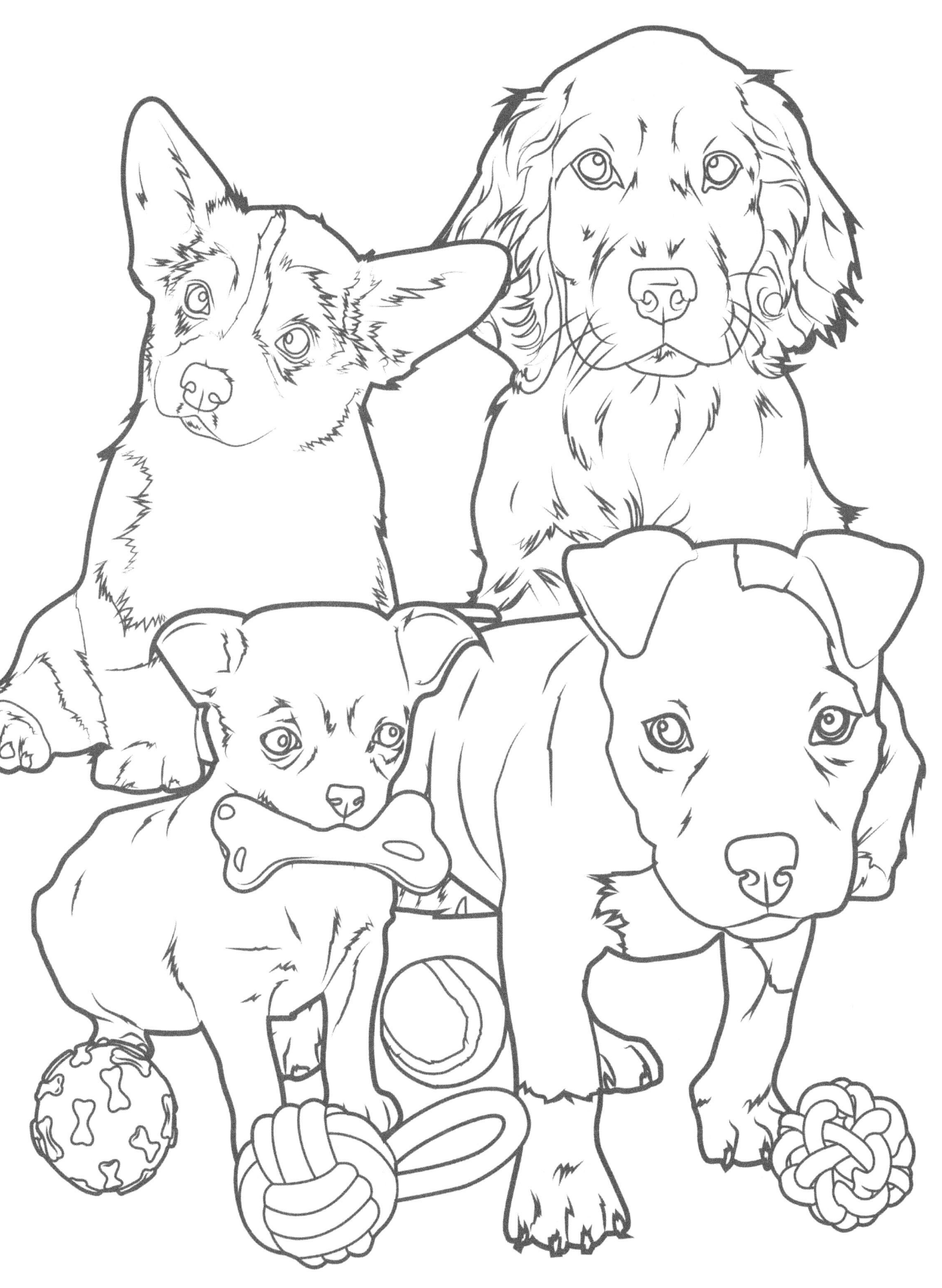

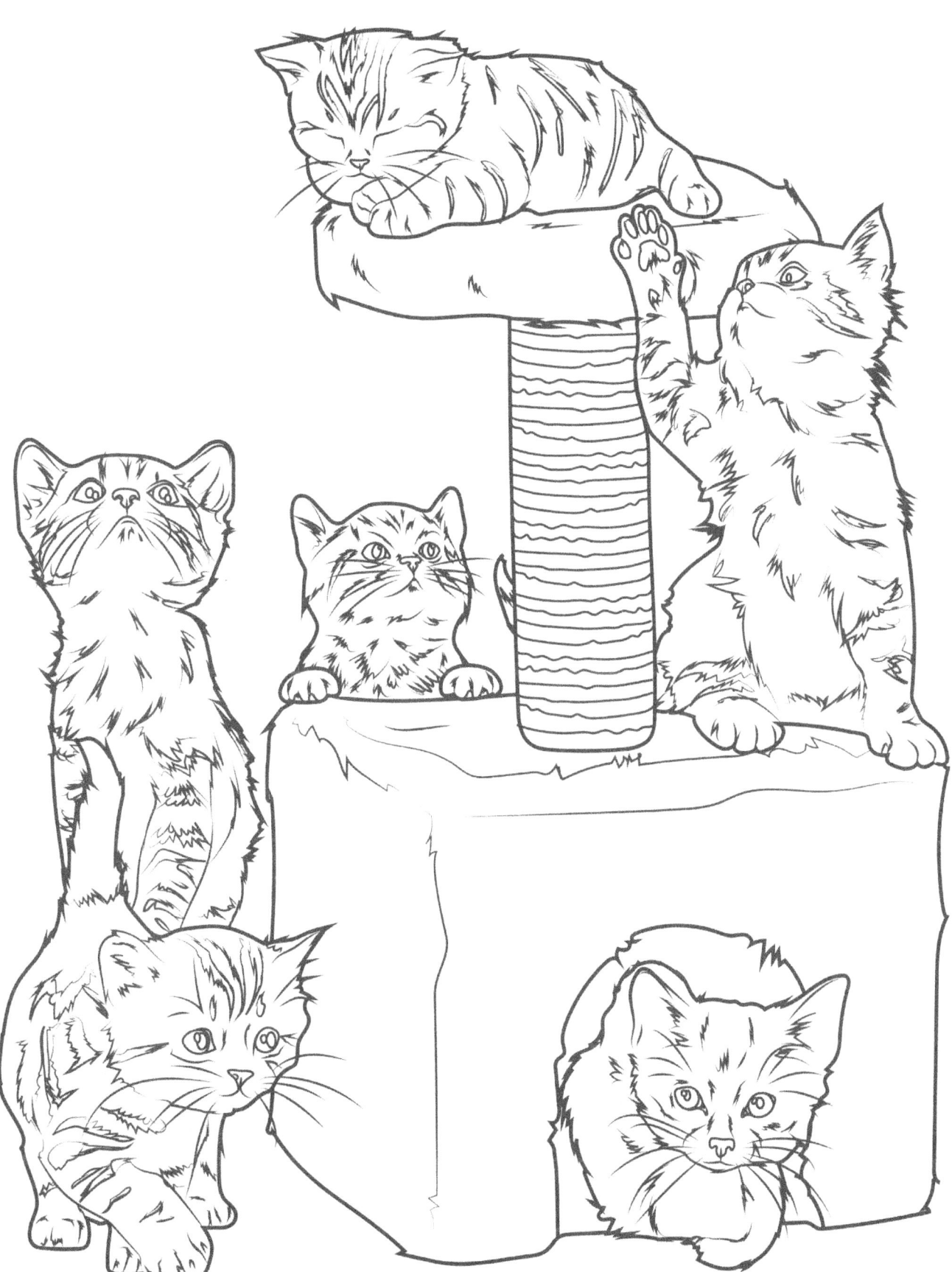

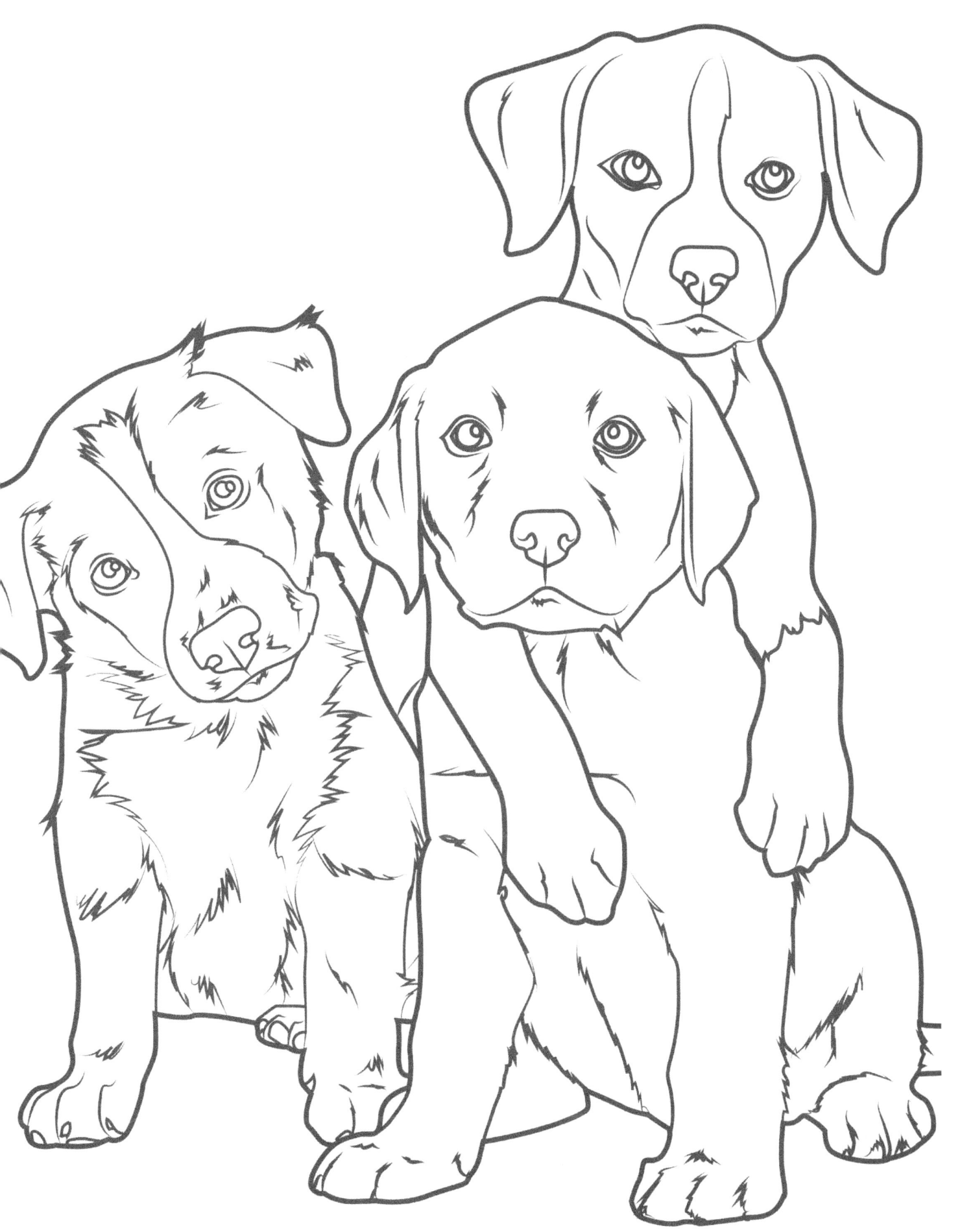

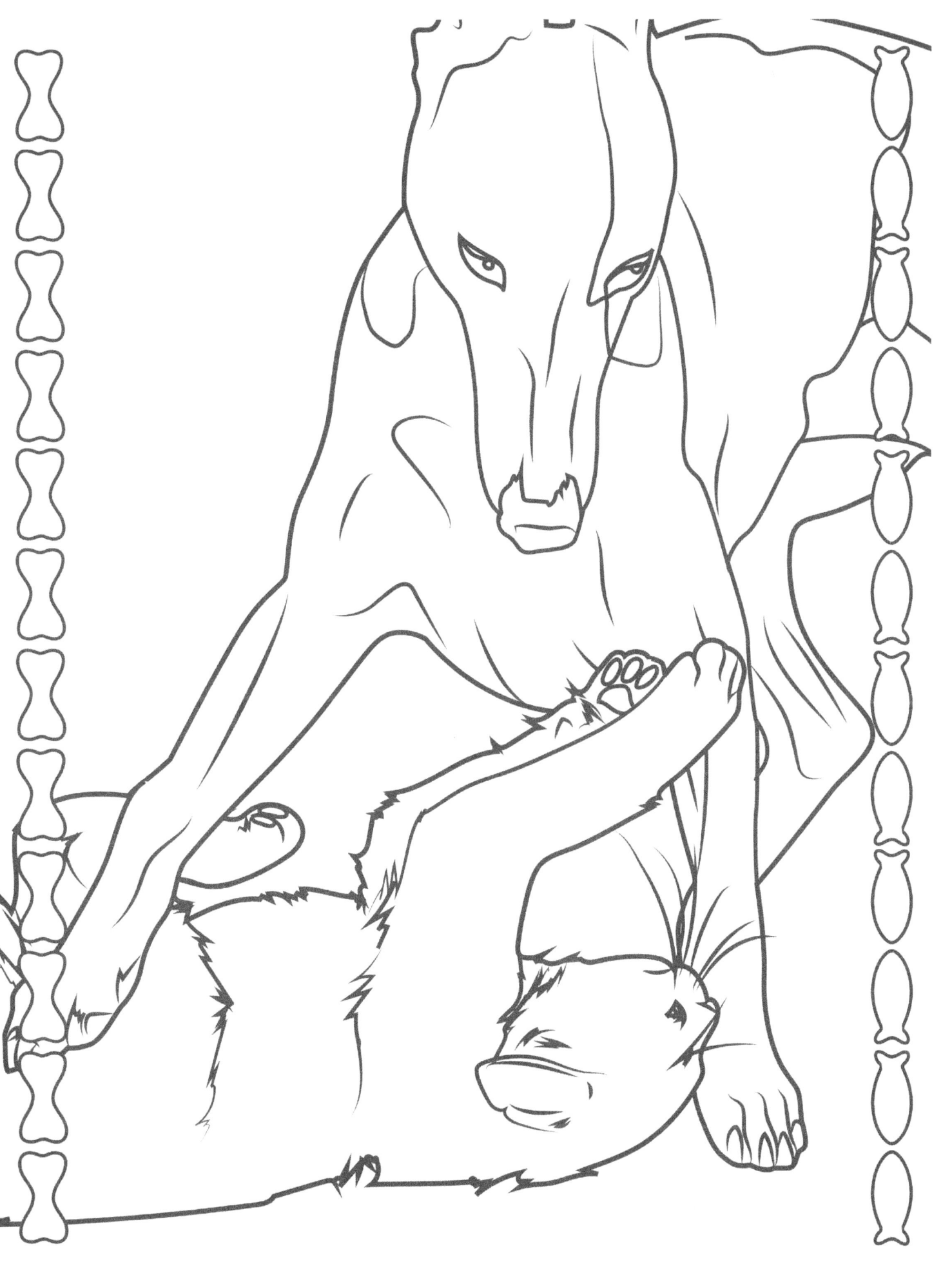

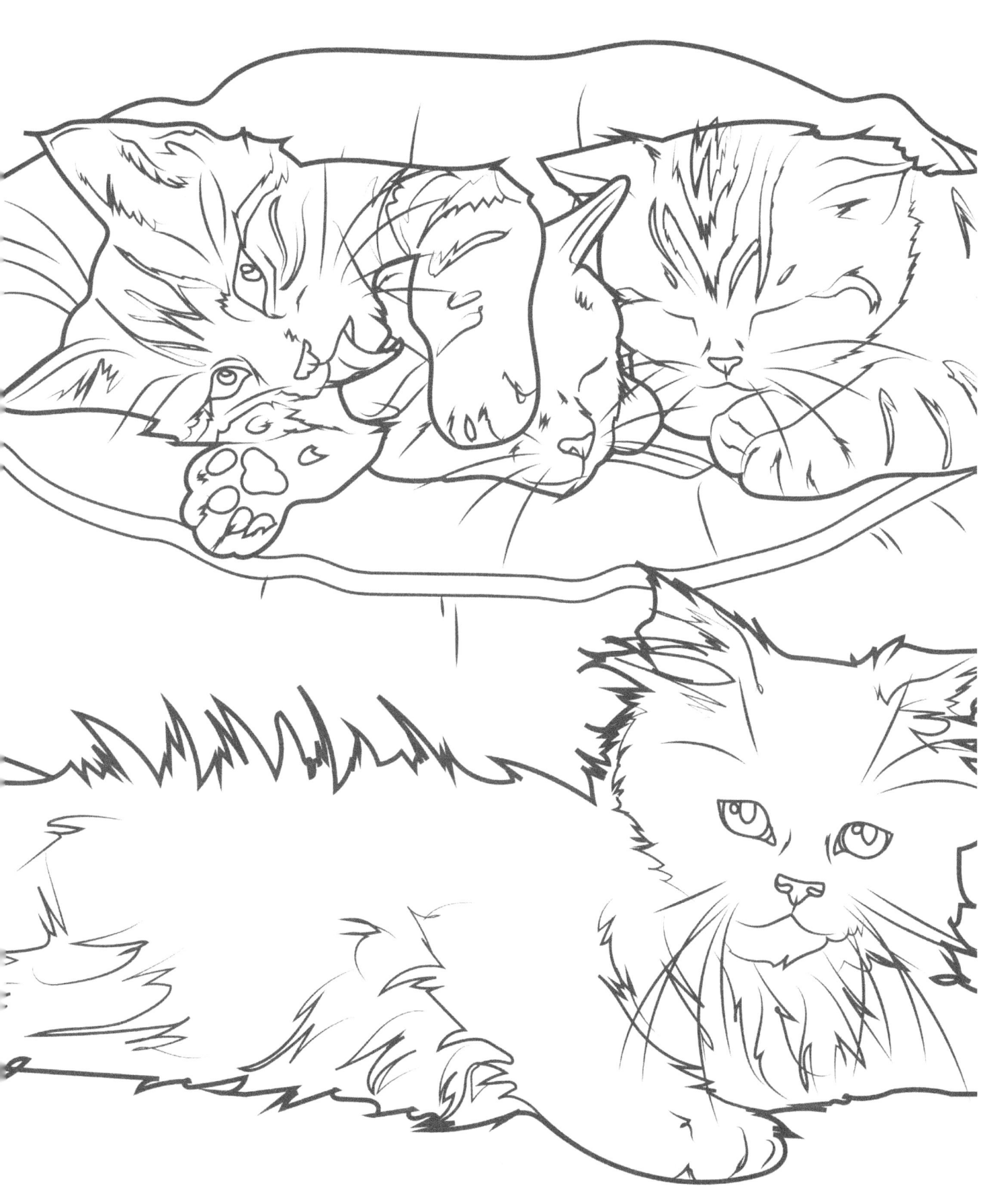

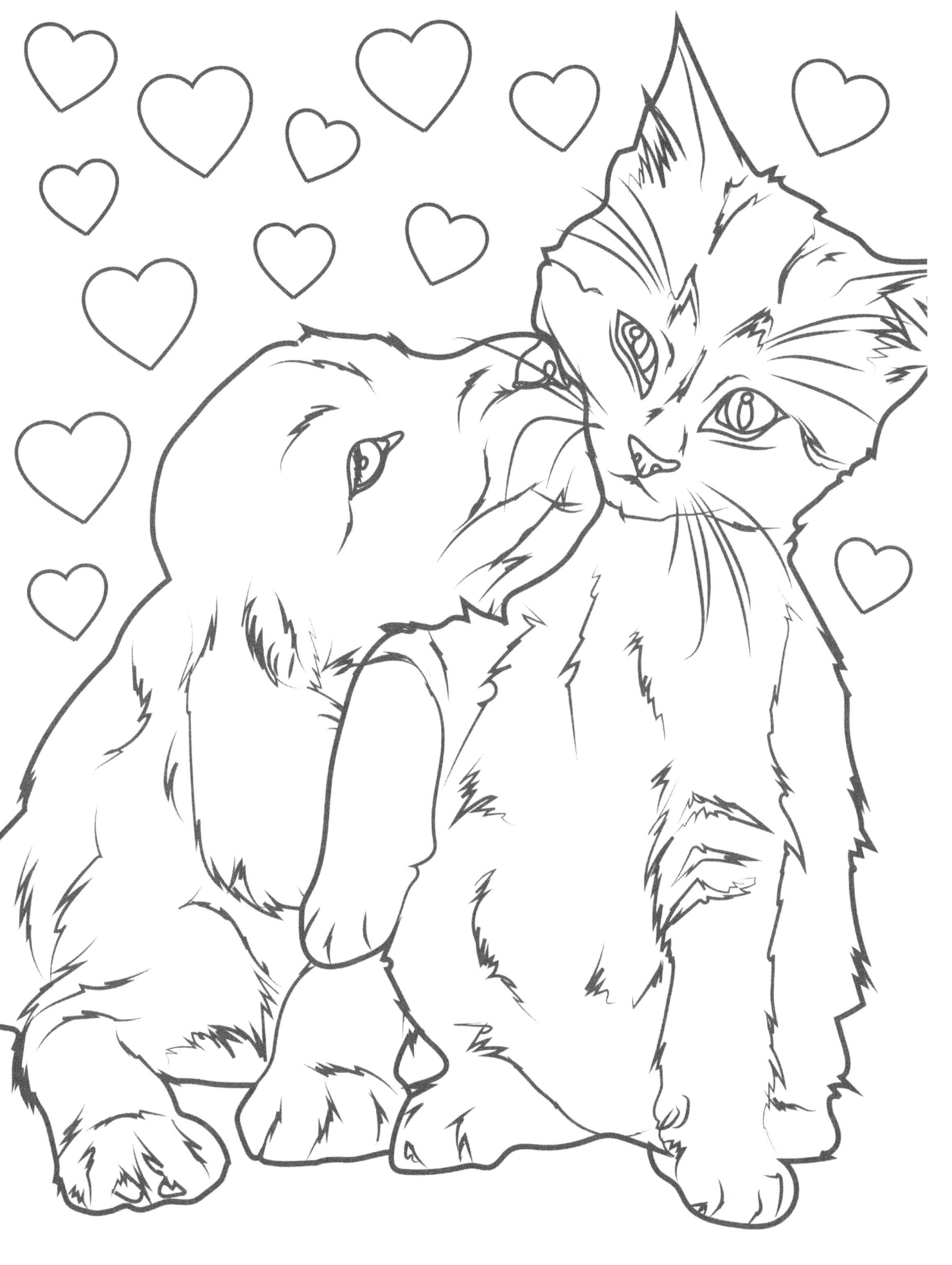

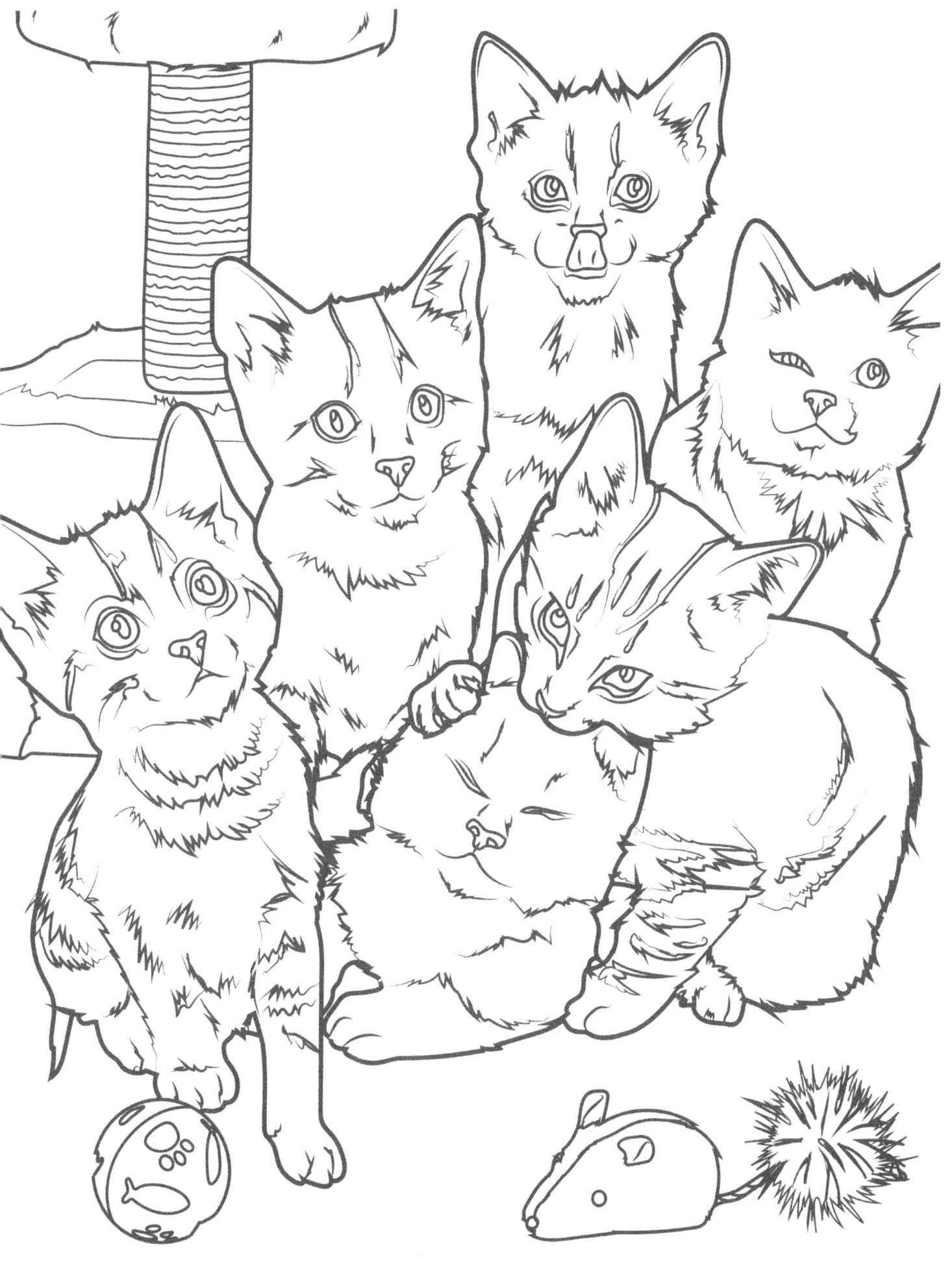

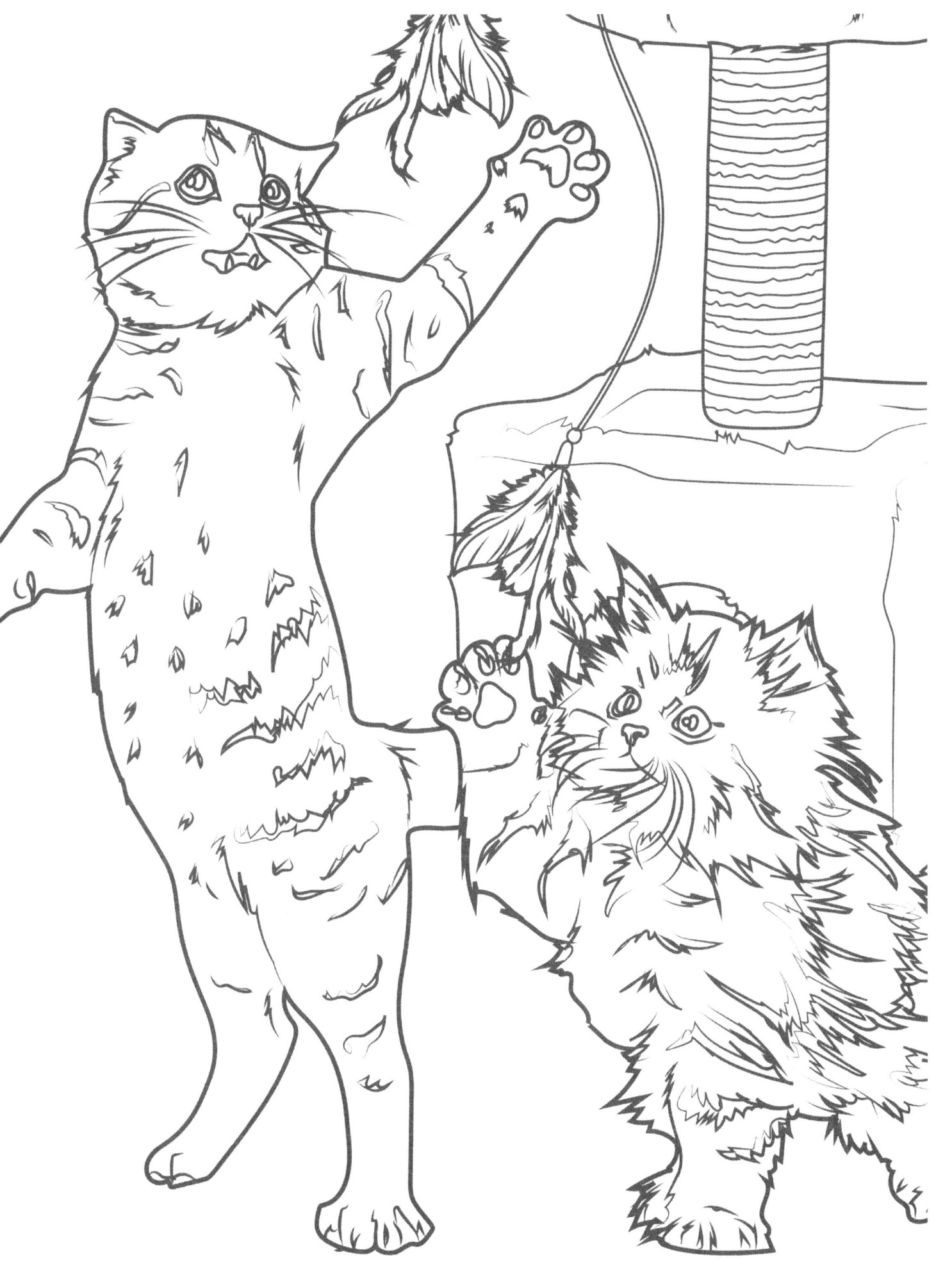

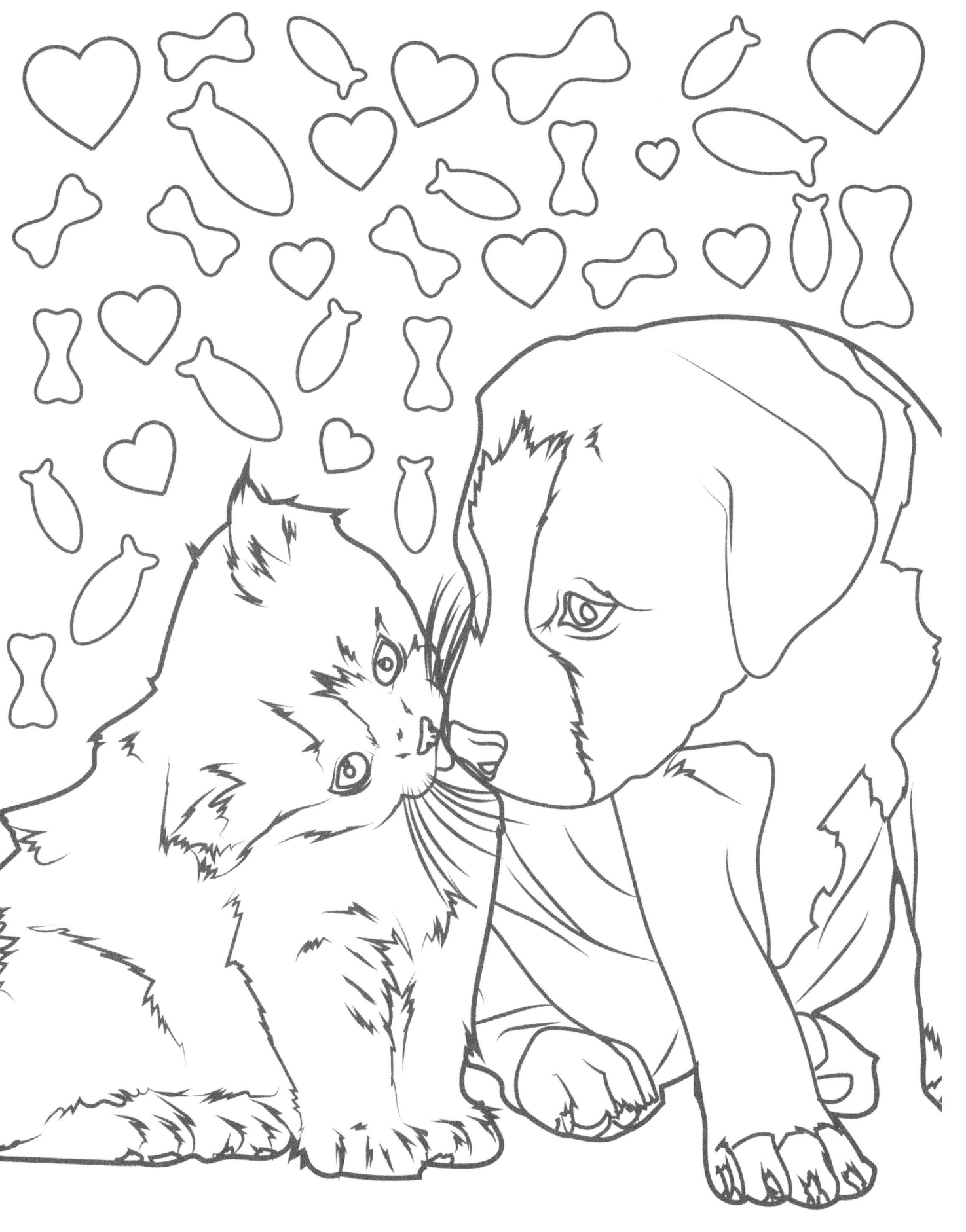

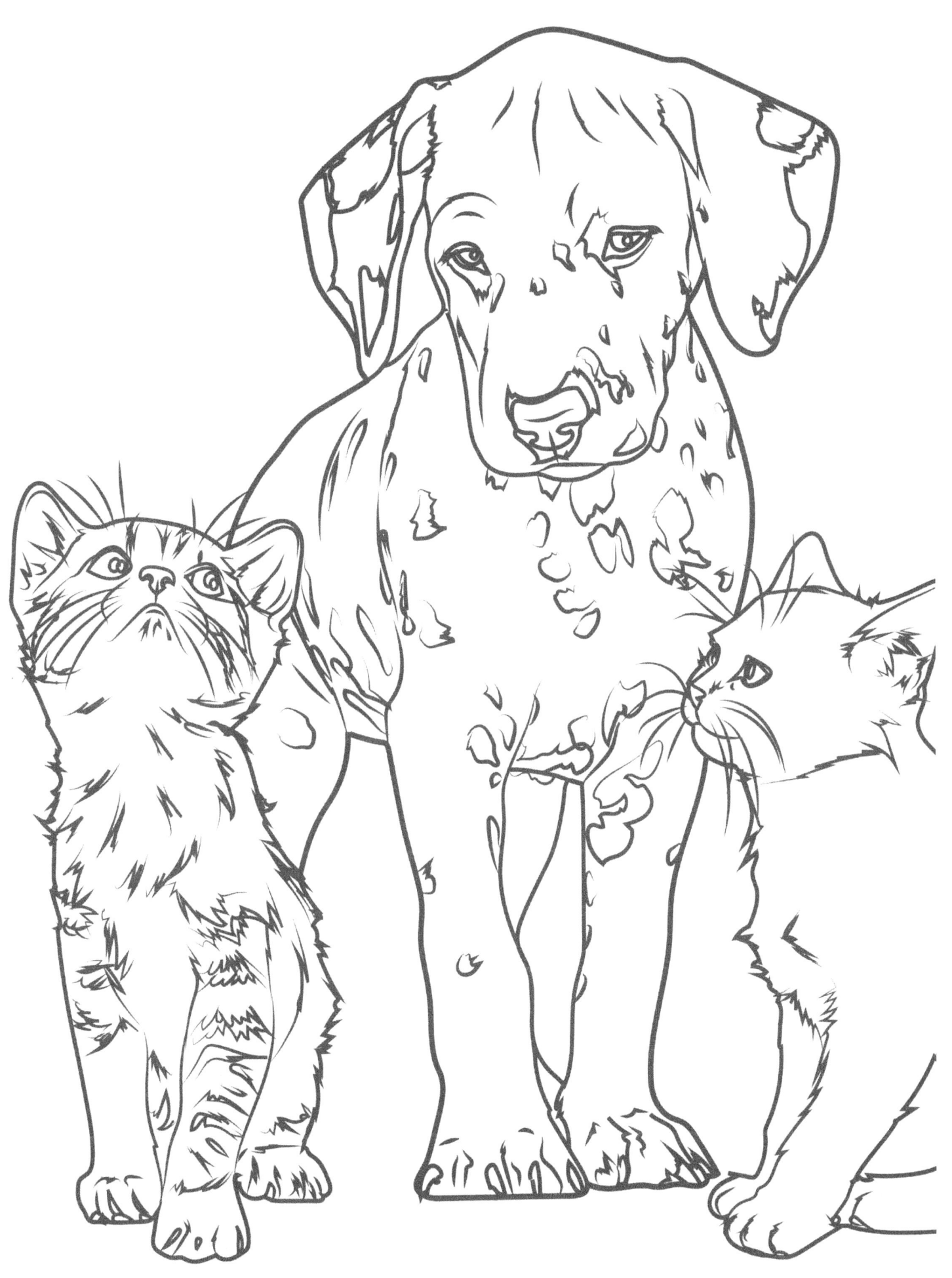

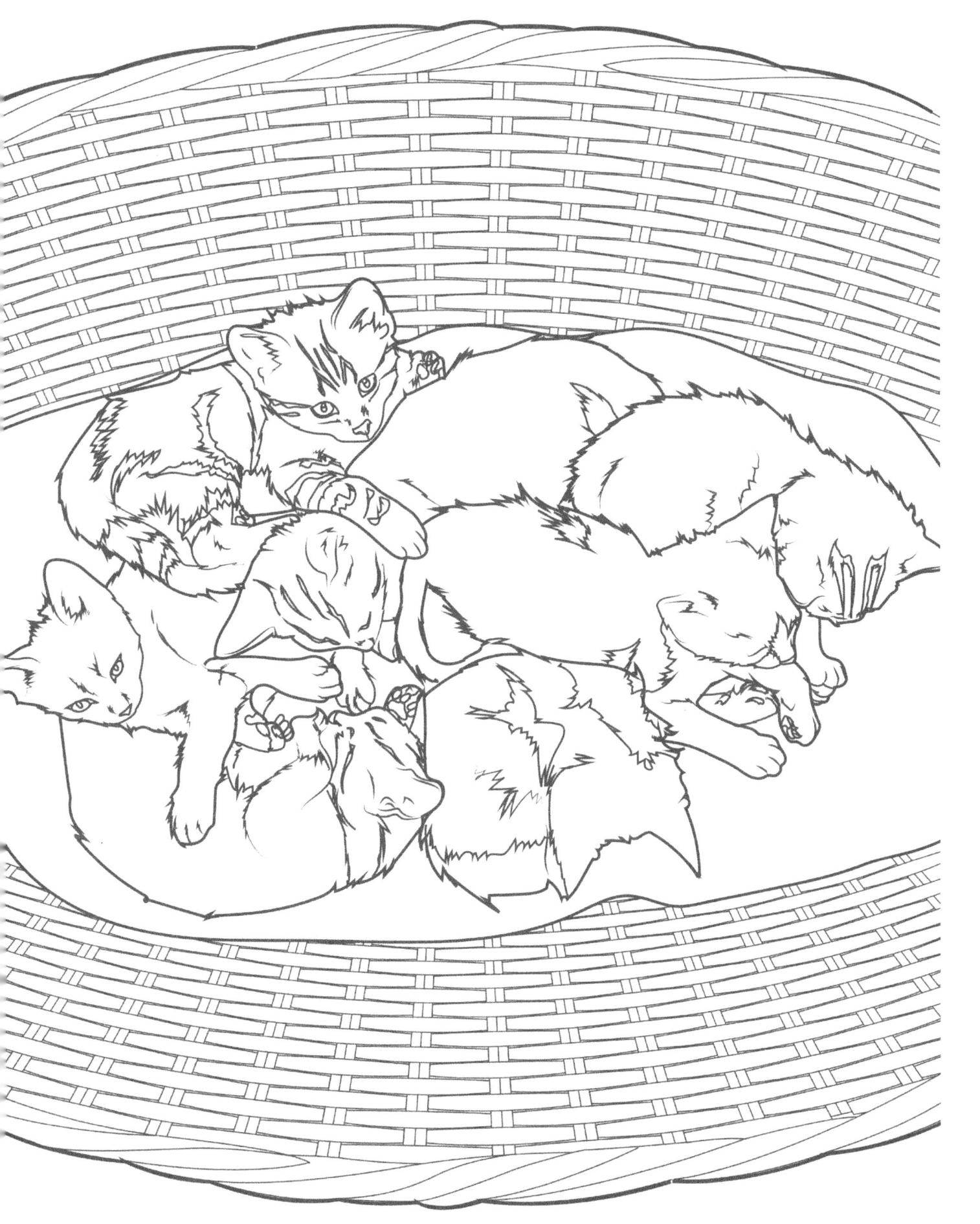

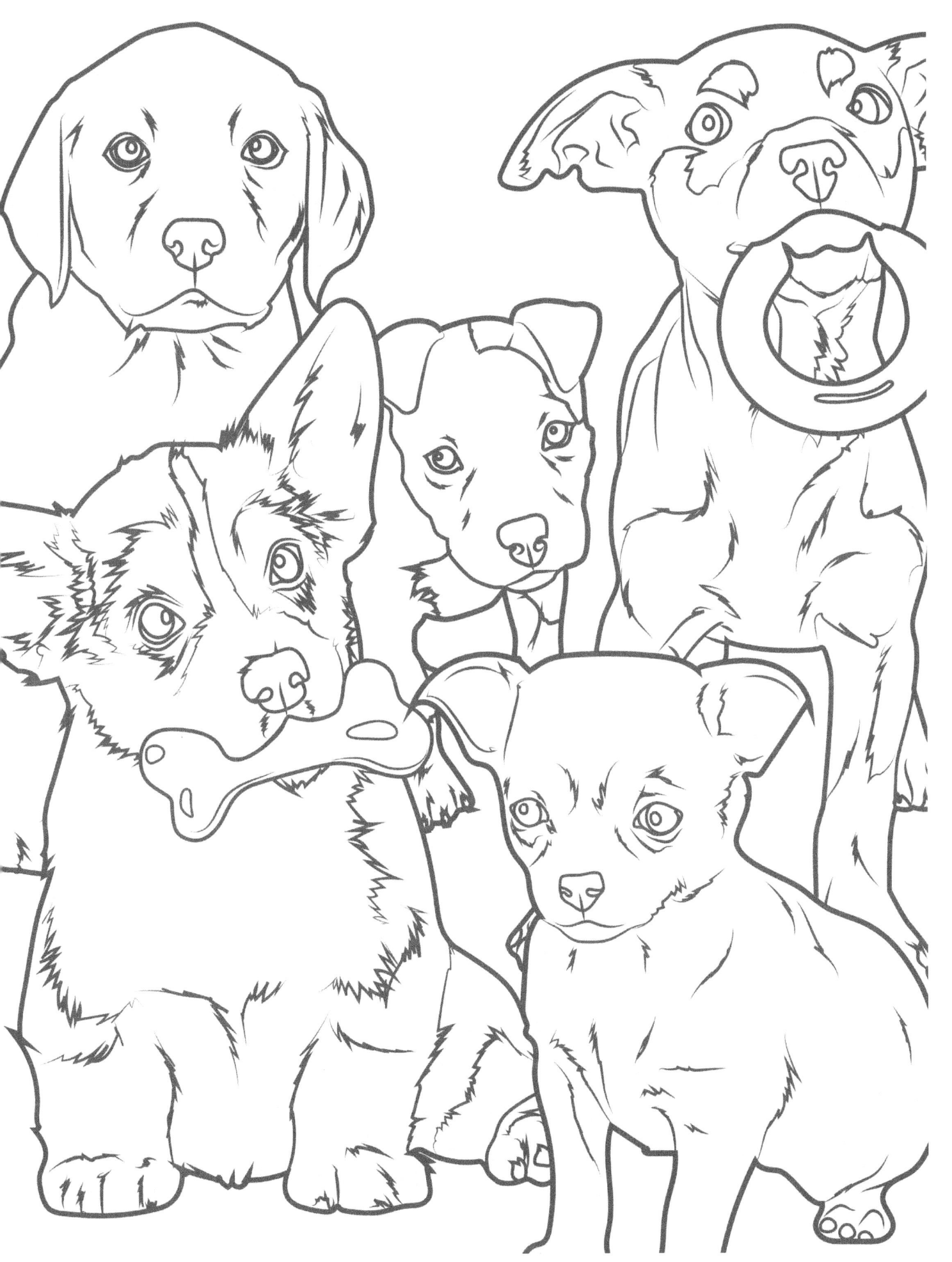

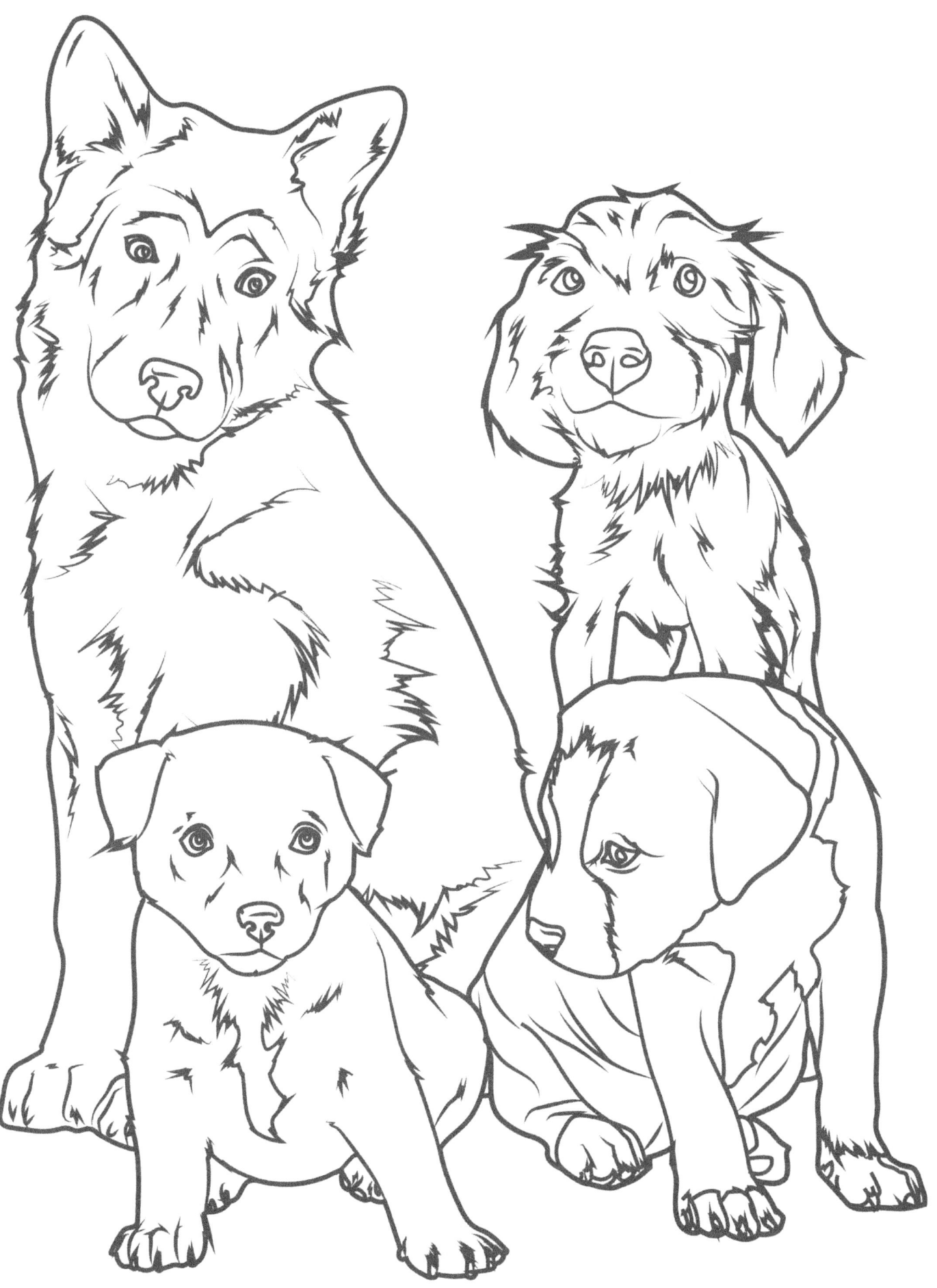

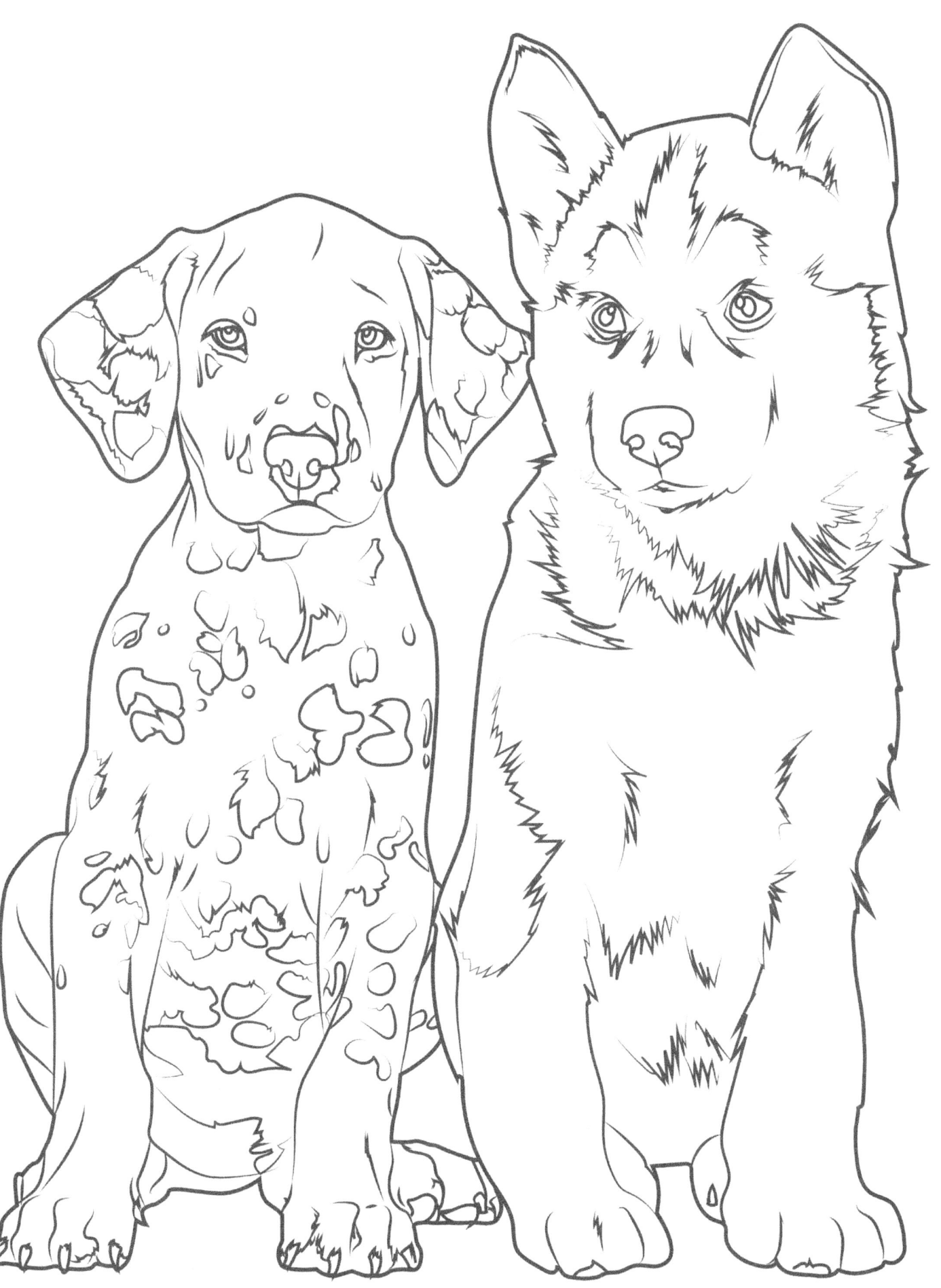

Thank you for purchasing this book.

If you would like to know more about Aryla Publishing Books please visit:-

www.ArylaPublishing.com

Or follow us on
Facebook
Twitter
Instagram
for *free promotions*

@arylapublishing

We would love to know what you think of this book so please leave us a review.

Have a wonderful day ☺

Other Coloring Books from Aryla Publishing

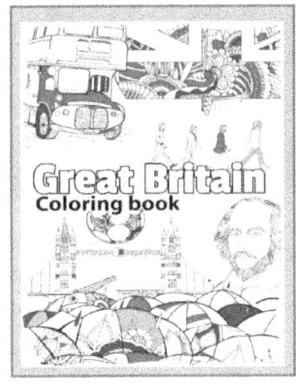
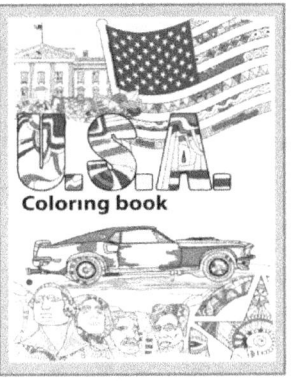
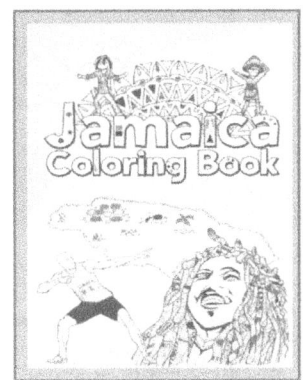
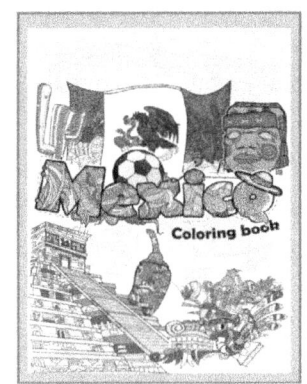

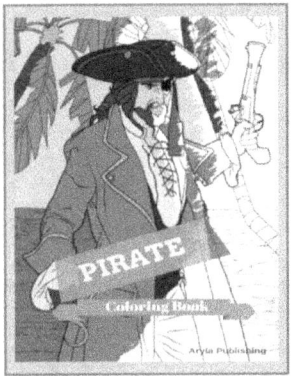
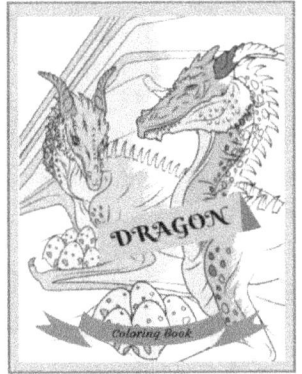
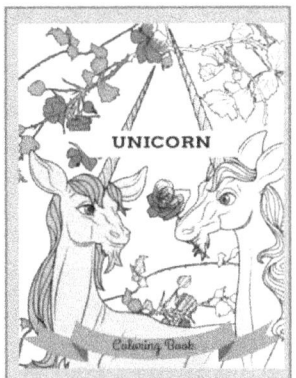
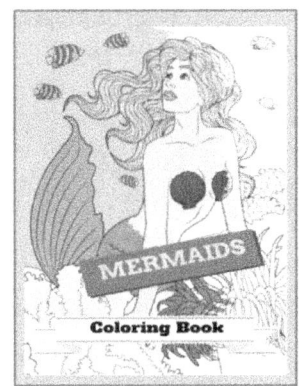

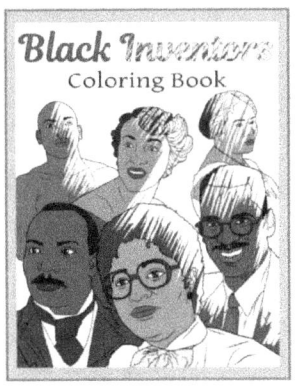
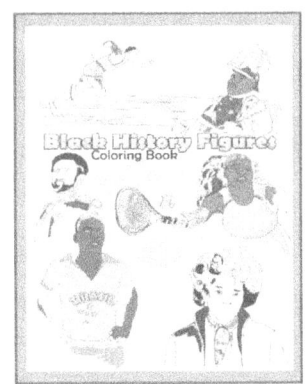
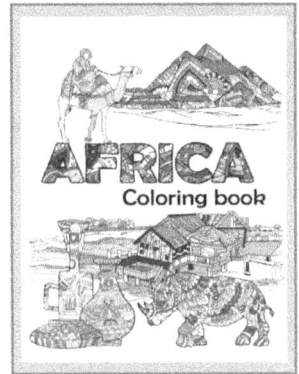
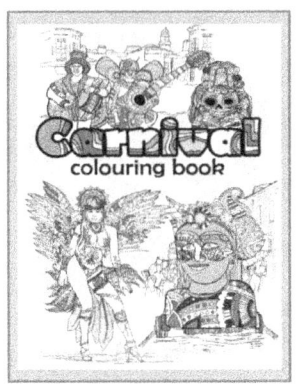

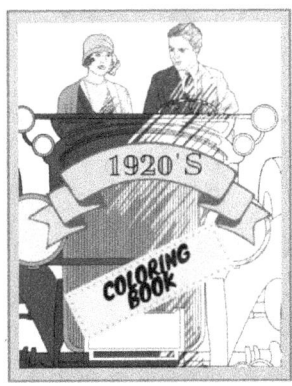
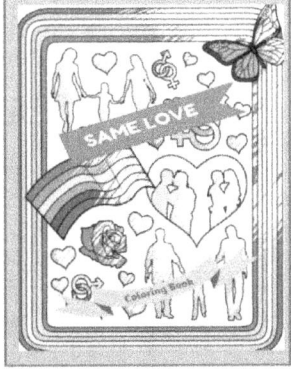
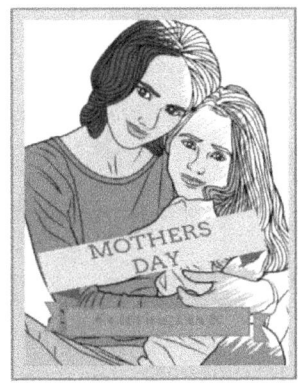
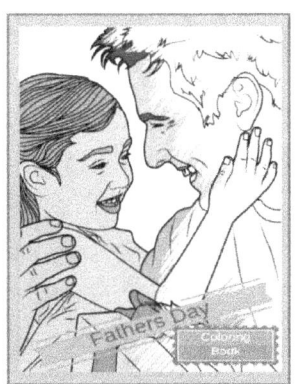

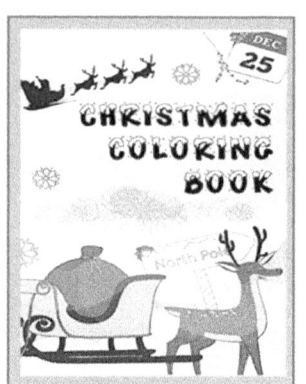
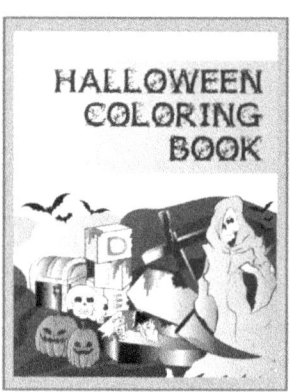
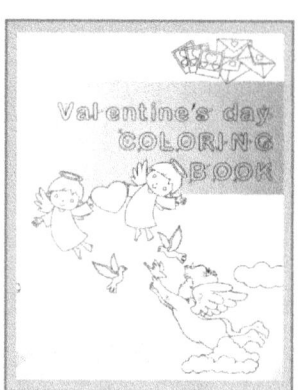
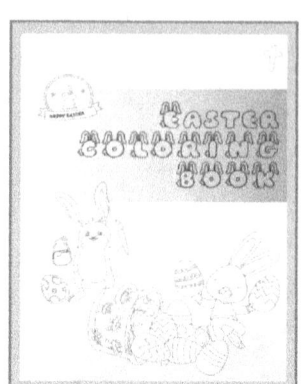

Visit **www.ArylaPublishing.com**
to find out about all new releases.

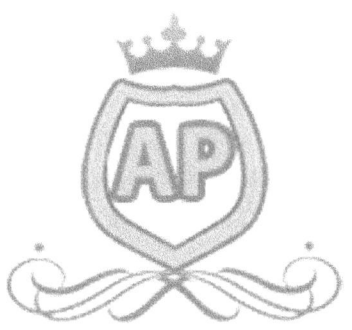

Follow us @arylapublishing on Twitter Instagram & Facebook

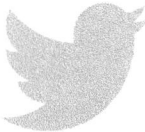  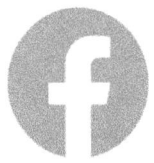

Search for Aryla Publishing on

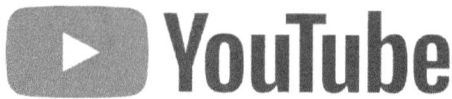 YouTube

Check out our <u>Book Trailers</u>

<u>Subscribe</u> **to keep up to date with new releases!**

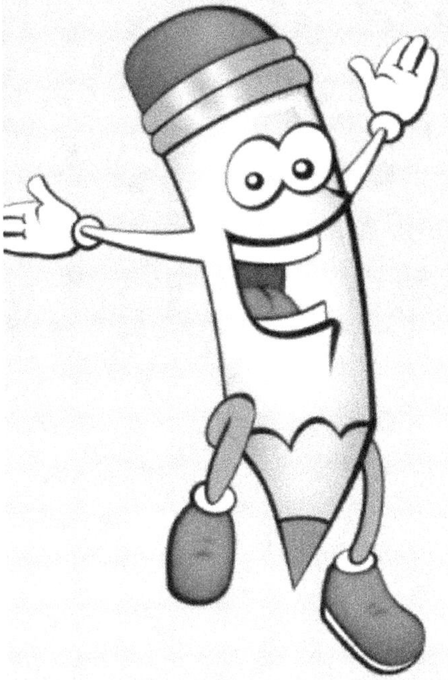

WE WOULD LOVE YOUR FEEDBACK

PLEASE LEAVE US A REVIEW AT:-

www.amazon.com/gp/product-review/

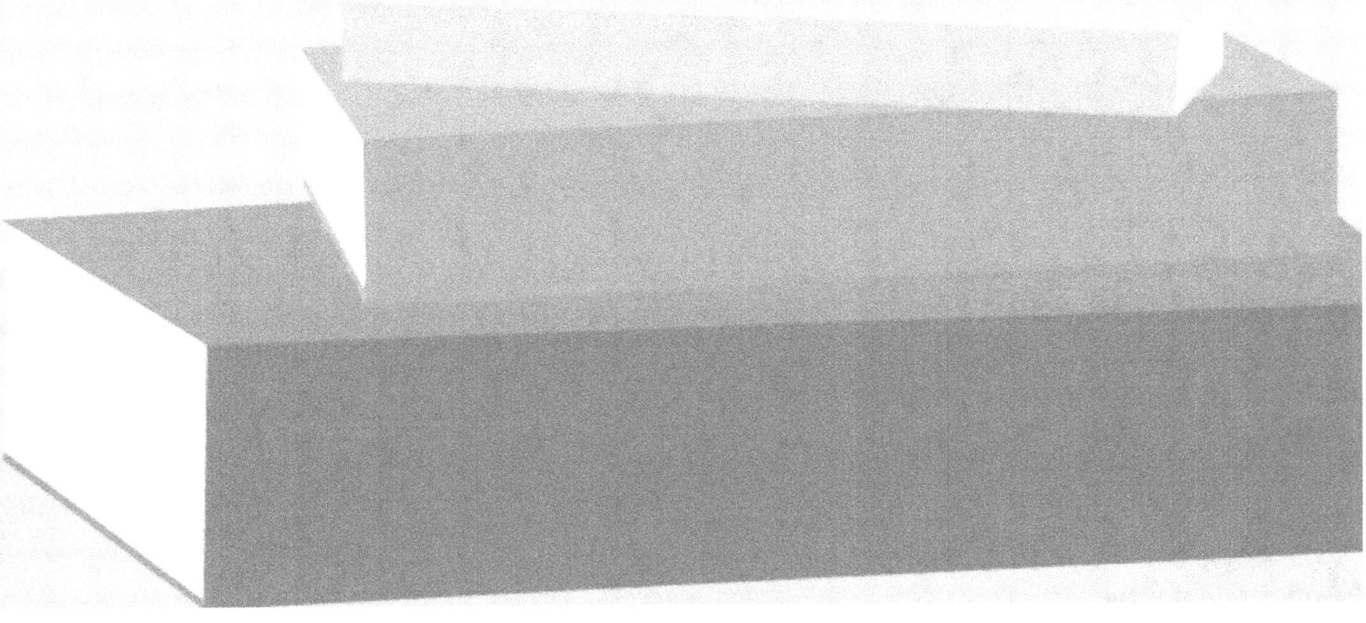